cupcakes

cupcakes

Phoebe Gibb

© 2012 Kerswell Farm Ltd

This edition published by King Books

Printed 2012

This book is distributed in the UK by
Parkham Books Ltd
Barns Farm, Boraston
Tenbury Wells
Worcestershire
WR15 8NB

david@kingbooks.co.uk

ISBN: 978-1-906239-87-9

DS0253. Cupcakes

Creative Director: Sarah King
Project editor: Clare Haworth-Maden
Designer: Jade Sienkiewicz
Photography: Paul Stewart-Reed

This material is a selection from *Cupcakes, best ever recipes*

Printed in Singapore

1 3 5 7 9 10 8 6 4 2

Contents

Introduction

Introduction

It's amazing that something as simple as a cupcake can bring so much pleasure. Gorgeous, aromatic and delicious, cupcakes are back in vogue, with whole shops dedicated to them springing up everywhere.

From tiny tots to grown-ups, it's hard to imagine anyone refusing one. Easy to make, they are also versatile, and can vary from a simple, coffee-time treat to a chic dessert for a dinner party. The aroma of freshly baked cupcakes is so delicious that it seems to turn a house into a home, and often brings back early childhood memories.

What is a cupcake? According to the dictionary, a cupcake is 'a small round cake baked in a foil or paper case'. Cupcakes date back to the early 1800s, when people first started measuring ingredients in cups.

Cakes were once frequently baked in small containers, such as teacups. Cupcakes have grown in popularity because they are so easy to make and can be as simple or as complicated as you like. Delicious in their most simple form, they can also be decorated in the most intricate ways, thanks to the huge number of different cake decorations available.

Children love baking, so why not get the whole family involved? Children enjoy every aspect of it, from preparing the mix to making the icing and drizzling it over the top, and especially making free with decorations, such as sprinkles. It can get a little messy at times, but it's usually worth it.

Cupcakes also make uniquely personal gifts, especially if they are presented in a special box or are wrapped in cellophane and decorated with ribbons. The look of sheer pleasure and delight on the face of the lucky recipient will be completely rewarding, and will make the effort really worthwhile.

There is a cupcake to suit everybody's taste in this book, so whether you love chocolate, prefer a healthier fruit-and-nut combination, or are perhaps holding a party for the kids or are celebrating a special occasion, you will find a delicious recipe to match your needs.

Equipment

Simple kitchen baking equipment is all you really need. You probably have most items already, and if not, most good cooking shops or supermarkets can supply the rest.

Cupcake trays
Cupcake trays are generally available in three sizes. A standard tray has 12 medium-sized holes; a muffin tin will make large cupcakes; and mini-tins are available for baby cupcakes. There are several options on offer, from metal, non-stick trays, to bendy, silicone varieties that do not require paper liners.

Cupcake papers
A huge variety of cupcake papers is available, depending on how extravagant you are feeling. The standard cases are plain and white, but you can buy all sorts of colours, ranging from pretty pastels to metallic golds and silvers. Different sizes are also easy to obtain.

Mixing bowls
You will need one large mixing bowl. A smaller bowl is also useful for melting chocolate or making icing.

Palette knives
A small palette knife is useful for spreading icing over cupcakes.

Spoons
A large, wooden spoon is vital for mixing. Metal tablespoons are needed to fold in the flour, and dessertspoons and teaspoons are often used to measure the quantities of ingredients.

Sieves
A single large sieve is all that is required for sifting dry ingredients, such as flour and spices. You can also use a sieve to dust the surface of a cupcake with icing sugar, for example.

Scales and measuring jugs
Accurate weighing scales and measuring jugs are vital to ensure that you are using the correct weights and amounts of ingredients.

Wire racks
Wire racks are used to cool the cupcakes after they have been baked.

Other equipment

An electric mixer can prove a valuable time-saver. A balloon whisk is essential for whisking egg whites.

Piping bags and nozzles are useful for any decoration requiring icing.

A pastry brush is useful to brush on glazes, and the newer, silicone brushes are just as efficient as the more traditional variety.

A timer is invaluable in helping you to gauge the correct baking time

Ingredients

Butter

Butter is the best fat for making cupcakes. Both unsalted and salted butter are called for in the recipes, but where the type is not specified, use unsalted. The temperature of the butter is also an important consideration as it is much easier to use when softened, so take it out of the fridge half an hour before you need to use it.

Sugar and other sweeteners

Caster sugar is the most frequently used sugar in cupcake-making. The fine grains allow it to incorporate a lot of air, which makes it perfect for creaming with butter for a really fluffy texture. Granulated sugar has larger grains than caster sugar and is often used for a crunchy, sweet topping.

Brown sugar gives a richer, caramel/treacle flavour. Icing sugar is a very fine powder sugar that is used to dust cupcake tops, as well as to make icings and glazes.

Golden syrup is a by-product of the sugar-refining process. It adds a distinctive, sweet flavour and colour to baked products.

Flour

When using plain flour, select a grade 00 flour if possible because the finer the ingredients you use, the better the result. Self-raising flour contains raising agents that make cakes rise and spread when heated in an oven.

Rice flour or potato flour are good substitutes if you are baking for anyone who has a gluten or wheat intolerance.

Eggs

Eggs should be fresh and free range. Always use room-temperature eggs when baking.

Chocolate

Use a good-quality, plain chocolate that contains at least 70 per cent cocoa solids. It is worth buying a well-known brand rather than a cheaper, generic product. Some recipes call for milk or white chocolate – again, use the best brand that you can find.

Fruits

A wide range of dried fruit is readily available, including tropical fruits and berries. Dried fruit has a more intense flavour than fresh fruit. Choose fruits that are moist and plump. Candied and crystallised fruit are better purchased as whole pieces if possible, then you can finely dice them yourself.

Nuts

Many varieties of nuts are used in cupcakes. Buy them whole and chop them yourself. Store them in an airtight container to keep them fresh.

Spices

Spices are often added to cupcake recipes and are an easy way to add flavour and aroma. They don't last forever, though, so check to make sure that your bottles still contain fresh spices.

Vanilla extract

Whenever vanilla essence is called for in a recipe, try to use the far superior vanilla extract. It may cost more, but is far better than any imitation vanilla essences.

Basic techniques

Marbled cupcakes

Take two different-flavoured mixes (chocolate and vanilla, for example). Fill one-third of the cupcake case with one mix, and then fill another third with the other. Swirl gently together with a small knife.

Layered cupcakes

Take two different-flavoured mixes (chocolate and vanilla, for example). Fill one-third of the cupcake case with one mix, then fill another third with the other.

Tiered cupcakes

Tiered cupcakes are cupcakes made either from one flavour of mix or from different flavours of mixes. The finished cupcake is then sliced and filled with jam, butter icing or cream.

other information

Oven temperatures

Different recipes call for different oven temperatures, so please make sure that you follow the recipe exactly and use the correct temperature. Also allow enough time for your oven to warm up to the right temperature.

Oven temperatures tend to vary slightly from model to model, so always check a few minutes before the cupcakes are meant to be ready to avoid overcooking them.

Never cook more than two trays of cupcakes at a time as this could cause the oven temperature to drop.

Storage and transportation

Cupcakes will remain fresh for several days if kept in an airtight container. Filled cupcakes should be eaten as soon as possible after assembly, however. Plain cupcakes keep well in the freezer, and are best defrosted the night before you need them.

If you are transporting your cupcakes to a party or function, nothing will serve them better than a good, strong, plastic, airtight container. Gently arrange the cupcakes in layers on pieces of greaseproof paper, and then place these layers in the box.

As gifts, cupcakes can be placed in pretty presentation boxes or can be wrapped in cellophane and decorated with ribbons. But remember to handle them gently!

Special diets

Many people have a dietary intolerance to certain ingredients, such as gluten, dairy products or eggs, or an allergy to such foods as nuts. Diabetes is also on the increase, so many people require low-sugar alternatives.

But do not despair: there is no need to miss out on the occasional cupcake. There are many recipes that provide fantastic, healthy (and delicious) alternatives, and you'll find many of them in this book.

Icings and other decorations

Cupcakes are usually best decorated shortly before you need them. There are hundreds of different ways that you can ice them, and many more ways to decorate the icing, with items ranging from dried fruits and nuts to specialised sugar decorations sold by specialist kitchen shops. The only limit is your imagination. The following recipes are for a few basic icings.

Coloured icing

150g (6oz) icing sugar

2–3 tbsp water

3–4 drops of the food colouring of your choice.

Sift the icing sugar into a mixing bowl. Now add the water a little at a time, until you have a smooth and shiny, but not runny, consistency. Add the food colouring of your preference and mix well.

Flavoured icing

150g (6oz) icing sugar

2–3 tbsp of your required flavouring (lemon juice, orange juice, brandy, liqueur, rum etc)

Sift the icing sugar into a mixing bowl. Now add your chosen flavouring a little at a time, until you have a smooth and shiny, but not runny, consistency.

Chocolate icing

150g (6oz) icing sugar

1–2 tbsp cocoa powder

1 tsp butter, softened

3–4 tbsp water

Sift the icing sugar and cocoa powder into a mixing bowl. Add the softened butter and water, stirring constantly until you have a smooth and shiny consistency.

Buttercream

75g (3oz) unsalted butter, softened

175g (7oz) icing sugar, sieved

2 drops vanilla extract

1–2 tbsp water

Put the butter in a bowl and beat with a wooden spoon until pale and fluffy. Gradually stir in the icing sugar, vanilla extract and water. Beat well until light and smooth.

Chocolate ganache

150ml (¼ pt) double cream

125g (5oz) plain or milk chocolate, broken into pieces.

Pour the cream into a small pan and bring to the boil. Remove from the heat and add the chocolate. Stir gently until the chocolate has melted and the mixture is smooth.

Return the mixture to the heat and bring to the boil. Remove immediately from the heat and allow to cool. Use at room temperature.

Coloured sugars

50g (2oz) caster sugar

3–4 drops of the food colouring of your choice

Place the caster sugar in a jar with a secure lid. Add the food colouring of your choice.

Tighten the lid and shake for a couple of minutes, until the sugar is evenly coloured.

Use the coloured sugar for decoration, to sprinkle over iced cupcakes.

Melting chocolate

There are two main methods to use when it comes to melting chocolate.

1 Melt chocolate on top of the hob by breaking it into small pieces and placing it in a heatproof bowl that fits over the top of a small saucepan. Put a small amount of water in the bottom of the saucepan and bring it to a simmer, then place the bowl containing the chocolate over the top. Reduce the heat and stir the chocolate until it has completely melted and is smooth and glossy in consistency.

2 Melt chocolate in the microwave by first placing the chocolate pieces in a microwave-safe bowl. Microwave on medium power for 1 minute and then stir. Repeat the process, stirring again after every 30 seconds until the chocolate has melted.

Classic cupcakes

Baby cupcakes

Baby cupcakes make perfect presents. Place three or four in a pretty box adorned with a few ribbons. Makes 24.

Ingredients

110g (4½oz) unsalted butter, softened
110g (4½oz) caster sugar
2 eggs
1 vanilla pod, deseeded
110g (4½oz) self-raising flour
A little milk

Icing

1 egg white
180g (7½oz) icing sugar, sifted
1 tsp lemon juice
Pink and yellow food colouring

Decorate

Dolly-mixture sweets

1   Pre-heat the oven to 180°C (350°F/Gas 4), then line a 24-hole mini-bun tin with paper cases.

2   In a bowl, cream the butter and sugar together until pale and creamy. Gradually beat in the eggs, a little at a time, beating well after each addition. Add the seeds from the vanilla pod, mixing well. Fold in the flour using a metal spoon. If the mixture is a little stiff, add a couple of spoonfuls of milk to create a better dropping consistency. Spoon this mixture into the prepared cases. Bake for 15–20 minutes until well risen and golden. Remove from the oven and transfer to a wire rack to cool.

3   For the icing, put the egg white in a bowl and gradually beat in the icing sugar, then the lemon juice, until thick and glossy. Divide into two bowls and tint one with the pink colouring and one with the yellow, to give the most delicate of pastel colours.

4   Spoon the topping on to the cupcakes and decorate with some dolly-mixture sweets.

Banana & caramel cupcakes

A totally indulgent sweet treat. Makes 12.

Ingredients

80g (3oz) butter
180g (7½oz) soft brown sugar
2 eggs, beaten
450g (1lb) bananas, mashed
200g (8oz) self-raising flour
¼ tsp bicarbonate of soda

Caramel sauce

1 can condensed milk

Decoration

1 banana, sliced
Lemon juice
175ml (6fl oz) double cream, whipped
Milk chocolate, grated

1 To make the caramel sauce, place a sealed can of condensed milk in a saucepan and pour over boiling water to cover the can. Boil for three hours, making sure that the can is always completely covered with water. Remove the can from the water and leave to cool completely before opening with a can opener. Stir well.

2 Pre-heat the oven to 180°C (350°F/Gas 4), then line a 12-hole bun tin with paper cases.

3 Cream the butter and sugar together until fluffy. Gradually beat in the eggs, a little at a time, beating well after each addition. Add the bananas and beat again. Fold in the flour and bicarbonate of soda with a metal spoon.

4 Spoon this mixture into the prepared cases and bake for 15–20 minutes until well risen and firm to the touch. Remove from the oven and transfer to a wire rack to cool.

5 Slice the banana and dip the slices into the lemon juice to avoid discolouration. Top each cake with a dollop of whipped cream and place a couple of slices of banana on top. Spoon over some of the caramel sauce and finally sprinkle with the grated chocolate. Eat straightaway.

Carrot cupcakes

This recipe is a great alternative to the very popular carrot cake.
Makes 12.

Ingredients

210g (8½oz) butter, softened
210g (8½oz) caster sugar
4 eggs
210g (8½oz) self-raising flour
1 tsp baking powder
½ tsp allspice
Grated zest of 1 orange
1 tbsp lemon juice

325g (13oz) carrots, peeled and grated
125g (5oz) chopped nuts

Icing

160g (6½oz) mascarpone
1 tsp orange zest, finely grated
1 tbsp orange juice
60g (2½oz) icing sugar

1   Pre-heat the oven to 180°C (350°F/Gas 4), then line a 12-hole bun tin with paper cases.

2   Cream the butter and sugar together until pale and creamy. Gradually beat in the eggs, a little at a time, beating well after each addition. Sift the flour, baking powder and allspice into the bowl. Add the orange zest and lemon juice; stir well. Add the carrots and chopped nuts; mix well.

3   Spoon this mixture into the prepared cases and bake for 15–20 minutes until well risen and golden. Remove from the oven and then transfer to a wire rack to cool.

4   For the icing, beat the mascarpone, orange zest, orange juice and icing sugar together until smooth. Spoon on to the cupcakes and serve.

Fig & cinnamon-topped cupcakes

If you like figs, you will love these. Makes 12.

Ingredients

100g (4oz) butter
100g (4oz) caster sugar
2 eggs, beaten
100g (4oz) self-raising flour

Topping

375g (15oz) dried figs
1 cinnamon stick
125g (5oz) caster sugar

1 Pre-heat the oven to 200°C (400°F/Gas 6), then line a 12-hole bun tin with paper cases.

2 To make the topping, place the dried figs, cinnamon stick, sugar and 370ml (13fl oz) boiling water in a saucepan, mix and bring to the boil. Reduce the heat and simmer for 20 minutes, or until the figs are soft and the water has reduced by a third. Remove the cinnamon stick and process in a food processor until smooth.

3 To make the cakes, cream the butter and sugar until pale and fluffy. Add the eggs a little at a time, beating well after each addition. Using a metal spoon, fold in the flour. If the mixture is too dry, add a little milk to make it a soft, dropping consistency. Alternatively, put all of the ingredients (apart from the milk) into a food processor, whizz until smooth, then add the milk.

4 Spoon the mixture into the paper cases, bake for 10 minutes, then remove from the oven. Spoon the fig mixture over the cakes and return to the oven for a further 10 minutes. Transfer to a wire rack to cool.

Fudge cupcakes

You can use shop-bought fudge, but make your own if you can.
Makes 12.

Ingredients
110g (4½oz) unsalted butter, softened
110g (4½oz) caster sugar
2 eggs, beaten
½ tsp vanilla essence
110g (4½oz) self-raising flour
A little milk
60g (2½oz) fudge sweets, roughly chopped

Fudge icing
50g (2oz) butter
125g (5oz) soft brown sugar
30ml (2 tbsp) whole milk
200g (8oz) icing sugar, sifted

Decoration
Fudge sweets, roughly chopped

1   Pre-heat the oven to 180°C (350°F/Gas 4), then line a 12-hole bun tin with paper cases.

2   Cream the butter and sugar together until pale and creamy. Gradually beat in the eggs, a little at a time, beating well after each addition. Add the vanilla essence. Fold in the flour using a metal spoon. If the mixture is a little stiff, add a couple of spoonfuls of milk to create a better dropping consistency. Finally, add the chopped fudge and mix well.

3   Spoon this mixture into the prepared cases and bake for 15–20 minutes until well risen and golden. Remove from the oven and transfer to a wire rack to cool.

4   To make the icing, put the butter, sugar and milk into a saucepan. Heat gently until the sugar dissolves, then bring to the boil and boil rapidly for 3–4 minutes. Remove from the heat and gradually stir in the icing sugar. Beat with a spoon until smooth. Use straightaway. Spoon on to the cupcakes and spread with a wet palette knife. Decorate with pieces of chopped fudge.

Glacé-fruit cupcakes

A truly colourful cupcake. Makes 12.

Ingredients

100g (4oz) butter, softened
100g (4oz) caster sugar
2 eggs
1 tsp vanilla essence
30g (1½oz) plain flour, sifted
30g (1½oz) self-raising flour, sifted
230g (9½oz) roughly chopped mixed glacé fruit

125g (5oz) mixed toasted nuts
25g (1oz) milk powder
2 tbsp brandy

Decorate

100g (4oz) icing sugar
1 tbsp water
A few drops of almond essence

1   Pre-heat the oven to 180°C (350°F/Gas 4), then line a 12-hole bun tin with paper cases.

2   Cream the butter and sugar together until pale and creamy. Gradually beat in the eggs, a little at a time, beating well after each addition. Add the vanilla essence, mixing well. Fold in the flour, fruit mixture, nuts, milk powder and brandy, using a metal spoon. If the mixture is too stiff, add a couple of spoonfuls of milk for a better dropping consistency.

3   Spoon this mixture into the prepared cases and bake for 15–20 minutes until well risen and golden. Remove from the oven and transfer to a wire rack to cool.

4   To make the icing, mix the icing sugar, water and a couple of drops of almond essence to taste until the mixture is smooth and spreadable. Drizzle this mixture over the top of the cakes.

Lemon drizzle cupcakes

Zesty and scrumptious. Makes 12.

Ingredients

110g (4½oz) unsalted butter, softened
110g (4½oz) caster sugar
2 eggs, beaten
110g (4½oz) self-raising flour
Finely grated zest of 1 lemon

Drizzle topping

125g (5oz) granulated sugar
60ml (2fl oz) lemon juice

1   Pre-heat the oven to 180°C (350°F/Gas 4), then line a 12-hole bun tin with paper cases.

2   Cream the butter and sugar together until pale and creamy. Gradually beat in the eggs, a little at a time, beating well after each addition. Fold in the flour and lemon zest, using a metal spoon. If the mixture is stiff, add a couple of spoonfuls of milk for a better dropping consistency.

3   Spoon this mixture into the prepared cases and bake for 15–20 minutes until well risen and golden. Remove from the oven and transfer to a wire rack. Whilst the cakes are still hot, prepare the drizzle topping. Mix the sugar and lemon juice together, but do not let the sugar dissolve.

4   Prick the top of the hot cupcakes with a fork. Pour the lemon drizzle over the still hot cupcakes. The juice will sink into the sponge, leaving a crunchy sugar topping.

Lemon meringue cupcakes

Sharp lemon and crunchy meringue - a fantastic combination. Makes 10.

Ingredients
110 g (4½ oz) unsalted butter, softened
110 g (4½ oz) caster sugar
110 g (4½ oz) self-raising flour
2 eggs, beaten
1 lemon with the rind finely grated.
A little milk

Lemon curd
4 egg yolks
75 g (3 oz) caster sugar
1½ tsp finely grated lemon rind
65 ml lemon juice
40 g (1½ oz) butter

Meringue
4 egg whites
225 g (9 oz) icing sugar

1   Make the lemon curd. Put all the ingredients in a small heatproof bowl over a pan of simmering water, stirring until the mixture starts to thicken. When mixture is thick enough to cover the back of a spoon remove from the heat and leave to cool. Refrigerate until needed.

2   Pre-heat oven to 180°C (350°F/Gas 4). Line a 10-hole muffin tray with large paper cases.

3   Cream butter and sugar together until pale and creamy. Gradually beat in the eggs, beating well after each one. Add lemon rind, mixing well. Fold in flour using a metal spoon. If mixture is a little stiff, add a couple of spoonfuls of milk to create a better dropping consistency.

4   Spoon mixture into the prepared cases and bake for 20 minutes until well risen and golden. Remove from oven and transfer to a wire rack to cool.

5   When cool make a 2cm hole in the top of each cake and fill with the lemon curd. Increase the oven temperature to 200°C (400°F, Gas Mark 6)

6   For the meringue, whisk egg whites and icing sugar together in a heatproof bowl over a pan of gently simmering water. After about 10 minutes the mixture should be very shiny and thick. Remove from heat and continue to whisk for a further 5 minutes. Pipe meringue onto the top of the cupcakes, place cakes on baking tray and bake in the oven for 5 minutes or until the meringue has slightly browned. Leave to cool before serving.

Maple-syrup & pecan cupcakes

Use real maple syrup if possible. Makes 12.

Ingredients

110g (4½oz) unsalted butter, softened
60g (2½oz) caster sugar
2 eggs, beaten
50g (2oz) pecan nuts, roughly chopped
150ml (¼pt) maple syrup
110g (4½oz) self-raising flour

Maple buttercream

60g (2½oz) butter, softened
150g (6oz) icing sugar
3 tbsp maple syrup

Decoration

12 pecan-nut halves
Maple syrup

1   Pre-heat the oven to 180°C (350°F/Gas 4), then line a 12-hole bun tin with paper cases.

2   In a bowl, cream the butter and sugar together until pale and creamy. Gradually beat in the eggs, a little at a time, beating well after each addition. Add the chopped pecan nuts and maple syrup, mixing well. Fold in the flour, using a metal spoon. If the mixture is a little stiff, add a couple of spoonfuls of milk to create a better dropping consistency.

3   Spoon this mixture into the prepared cases and bake for 15–20 minutes until well risen and golden. Remove from the oven and transfer to a wire rack to cool.

4   For the buttercream, beat butter, icing sugar and maple syrup until fluffy.

5   Liberally spread the buttercream on to the cupcakes, add a pecan nut to each for decoration and drizzle with a little more maple syrup.

Marbled cupcakes

These are very easy to make. Makes 12.

Ingredients
110g (4½oz) unsalted butter, softened
110g (4½oz) caster sugar
2 eggs, beaten
110g (4½oz) self-raising flour
A little milk
½ tsp vanilla essence
1 tbsp cocoa powder, sifted

Chocolate buttercream
75g (3oz) butter, softened
175g (7oz) icing sugar, sifted
40g (1½oz) chocolate, melted

Decoration
Chocolate buttons

1 Pre-heat the oven to 180°C (350°F/Gas 4), then line a 12-hole bun tin with paper cases.

2 Cream the butter and sugar together until pale and creamy. Gradually beat in the eggs, a little at a time, beating well after each addition. Fold in the flour, using a metal spoon. If the mixture is a little stiff, add a couple of spoonfuls of milk to create a better dropping consistency. Divide this mixture into two, add the vanilla essence to one half, the sifted cocoa powder to the other half, and mix both well.

3 Spoon this mixture into the prepared cases, 1 teaspoonful at a time, alternating the mixes. They will not appear to be mixed, but will look marbled when cooked. Bake for 15–20 minutes until well risen and golden. Remove from the oven and transfer to a wire rack to cool.

4 Cream the butter until soft, then gradually beat in the icing sugar. Finally, add the melted chocolate and mix well.

5 Spoon the chocolate buttercream over the cupcakes and decorate with the chocolate buttons.

Pineapple & coconut cupcakes

A touch of the exotic Makes 12.

Ingredients

375g (15oz) self-raising flour
1 tsp cinnamon
375g (15oz) caster sugar
100g (4oz) desiccated coconut
5 eggs, beaten
440g (1lb) tin crushed pineapple in syrup
370ml (13fl oz) vegetable oil

Lemon icing

60g (2½oz) cream cheese
30g (1½oz) butter, softened
1 tbsp lemon juice
175g (7oz) icing sugar

Decoration

Desiccated coconut

1. Pre-heat the oven to 180°C (350°F, Gas 4), then line a 12-hole bun tin with paper cases.

2. In a large bowl, sift the flour and cinnamon, then add the sugar and coconut and mix well. Add the eggs, pineapple and oil. Mix well.

3. Spoon into the prepared cases and bake for 20–25 minutes. Transfer to a wire rack and then cool.

4. To make the lemon icing, put all of the ingredients into a bowl and beat until creamy and smooth.

5. Spread the icing over the top of the cupcakes and sprinkle with a little more desiccated coconut.

Pistachio cupcakes

A very delicately flavoured cupcake. Makes 12.

Ingredients

50g (2oz) pistachio nuts
110g (4½oz) unsalted butter, softened
110g (4½oz) caster sugar
2 eggs, beaten
110g (4½oz) self-raising flour

Icing

240g (9½oz) mascarpone cheese
10ml (2 tsp) lemon juice
110ml (4fl oz) coconut milk
120g (4½oz) icing sugar

Decoration

Pistachio nuts

1 Pre-heat the oven to 180°C (350°F/Gas 4), then line a 12-hole bun tin with paper cases.

2 Put the nuts in a food processor and process until finely ground.

3 In a bowl, cream the butter and sugar together until pale and creamy. Gradually beat in the eggs, a little at a time, beating well after each addition. Add the ground pistachio nuts, mixing well. Fold in the flour, using a metal spoon. If the mixture is a little stiff, add a couple of spoonfuls of milk to create a better dropping consistency.

4 Spoon this mixture into the prepared cases and bake for 15–20 minutes until well risen and golden. Remove from the oven and then transfer to a wire rack to cool.

5 To make the icing, put all of the ingredients into a bowl and whisk until smooth. Chill until thickened.

6 Liberally spread the icing on to the cupcakes and sprinkle with pistachio nuts.

Praline & coffee
iced cupcakes

The praline sounds complicated, but it's really easy to make – just ensure that you don't burn it.
Makes 12.

Ingredients

110g (4½oz) unsalted butter, softened
110g (4½oz) caster sugar
2 eggs, beaten
½ tsp vanilla essence
110g (4½oz) self-raising flour
A little milk

Coffee icing

1 egg white
175g (7oz) caster sugar

Pinch of salt
30ml (2 tbsp) water
Pinch of cream of tartar
1 tsp instant coffee dissolved in ½ tbsp
boiling water

Praline

65g (2½oz) caster sugar
50g (2oz) hazelnuts, roughly chopped and
slightly toasted

1. To make the praline, place the sugar in a dry pan and heat gently, stirring until the sugar has melted. Gently simmer for about 5 minutes, until pale gold. Add the hazelnuts and mix well. Pour the mixture on to a baking tray lined with grease-proof paper. Leave to set. When set, roughly break up the praline, place in a food processor and whizz briefly.

2. Pre-heat the oven to 180°C (350°F/Gas 4), then line a 12-hole bun tin with paper cases.

3. Cream the butter and sugar together until pale and creamy. Gradually beat in the eggs, a little at a time, beating well after each addition. Add the vanilla essence, mixing well. Fold in the flour, using a metal spoon. If the mixture is a little stiff, add a couple of spoonfuls of milk to create a better dropping consistency.

4. Spoon this mixture into the prepared cases and bake for 15–20 minutes until well risen and golden. Remove from the oven and transfer to a wire rack to cool.

5. To make the icing, put all of the ingredients (apart from the dissolved coffee) into a heatproof bowl and whisk lightly. Put the bowl over a pan of hot water and continue whisking for about 6 minutes, until the mixture is thick enough to hold peaks. Add the coffee and stir until thoroughly combined.

6. Spoon the icing over the cakes, then liberally sprinkle with the praline.

Rose cupcakes
with frosted petals

Simple and elegant. Makes 12.

Ingredients

110g (4½oz) unsalted butter, softened
110g (4½oz) caster sugar
2 eggs, beaten
1½ tbsp rosewater
110g (4½oz) self-raising flour

Icing

2 tbsp water
150g (6oz) icing sugar
Pink food colouring

Decoration

12 rose petals
1 egg white
2 tbsp caster sugar

1   Pre-heat the oven to 180°C (350°F/Gas 4), then line a 12-hole bun tin with paper cases.

2   Cream the butter and sugar together until pale and creamy. Gradually beat in the eggs, a little at a time, beating well after each addition. Add the rosewater, mixing well. Fold in the flour, using a metal spoon. If the mixture is a little stiff, add a couple of spoonfuls of milk to create a better dropping consistency.

3   Spoon this mixture into the prepared cases and bake for 15–20 minutes until well risen and golden. Remove from the oven and transfer to a wire rack to cool.

4   To make the frosted rose petals, dip them in the egg white and dust with the caster sugar. Leave to dry for approximately 1 hour.

5   To make the icing, put the water in a bowl and sift in the icing sugar. Mix until thoroughly combined, then add a couple of drops of pink food colouring and stir.

6   Spoon this on to the cakes and decorate each with one of the rose petals.

Summer berry & Chantilly cream cupcakes

The perfect al fresco cakes. Makes 12.

Ingredients

110g (4½oz) unsalted butter, softened
110g (4½oz) caster sugar
2 eggs, beaten
½ tsp vanilla essence
110g (4½oz) self-raising flour
A little milk

Chantilly cream

1 vanilla pod, deseeded
50g (2oz) icing sugar, sifted
180ml (6¼fl oz) double cream, whipped

Decoration

A mixture of fresh summer berries, such as
raspberries, blackcurrants,
strawberries and blueberries
Icing sugar

1 Pre-heat the oven to 180°C (350°F/Gas 4), then line a 12-hole bun tin with paper cases.

2 Cream the butter and sugar together until pale and creamy. Gradually beat in the eggs, a little at a time, beating well after each addition. Add the vanilla essence, mixing well. Fold in the flour, using a metal spoon. If the mixture is a little stiff, add a couple of spoonfuls of milk to create a better dropping consistency.

3 Spoon this mixture into the prepared cases and bake for 15–20 minutes until well risen and golden. Remove from the oven and transfer to a wire rack to cool.

4 To make the Chantilly cream, mix the vanilla pod and icing sugar into the whipped cream. Spoon the cream on to the cakes and decorate with summer berries. Finally, dust with icing sugar.

Filled cupcakes

Banoffee tower

Toffee and banana – who could resist? Makes 10.

Ingredients

75g (3oz) butter
175g (7oz) soft brown sugar
2 eggs, beaten
450g (1lb) bananas, mashed
200g (8oz) self-raising flour
¼ tsp bicarbonate of soda

Caramel sauce

1 can condensed milk

Decoration

3 bananas, sliced
Lemon juice
250ml (½pt) double cream, whipped
Milk chocolate, grated

1 To make the caramel sauce, place a sealed can of condensed milk in a saucepan and pour over boiling water to cover the can. Boil for 3 hours, making sure that the can is always completely covered with water. Remove the can from the water and leave to cool completely before opening with a can opener. Stir well.

2 Pre-heat the oven to 180°C (350°F/Gas 4), then line a muffin tin with large paper cases.

3 Cream butter and sugar together until fluffy. Gradually beat in the eggs, a little at a time, beating well after each addition. Add bananas and beat again. Fold in the flour and bicarbonate of soda with a metal spoon.

4 Spoon mixture into the prepared cases and bake for 20 minutes until well risen and firm to the touch. Remove from the oven and transfer to a wire rack to cool.

5 When cool, slice the cupcakes into three horizontal slices. Dip the banana slices into the lemon juice to avoid discolouration. Top each cupcake slice with a spoon-ful of caramel sauce, sliced banana and a spoonful of cream. Sandwich the slices together. Top each cake with a dollop of whipped cream. Finally, sprinkle with the grated chocolate. Eat straightaway.

Gingerbread & lemon cream

The spice of the ginger and the citrus of the lemon make a great combination. Makes 10.

Ingredients

60g (2½oz) unsalted butter
50g (2oz) soft brown sugar
3 tbsp golden syrup
1 tbsp treacle
1 tsp ground ginger
90ml (3fl oz) milk
1 egg, beaten
120g (4½oz) self-raising flour, sifted

Homemade lemon curd

2 eggs, beaten
Grated zest and juice of 2 lemons
50g (2oz) butter, cut into small pieces
150g (6oz) caster sugar
(Alternatively, use ready-made lemon curd)

Lemon cream

300ml (½pt) double cream
2 tbsp lemon curd from mixture above

Decoration

Finely grated rind of 1 lemon

1   Make the lemon curd. Place all of the ingredients in a large, heatproof bowl placed over a pan of simmering water. Stir until the mixture has dissolved and continue to heat gently for about 20 minutes, stirring all the time until mixture is thick enough to coat the back of a spoon. Do not allow mixture to boil. Strain mixture through a fine sieve into a clean bowl and set aside until ready to use.

2   Pre-heat the oven to 180°C (350°F/Gas 4), then line a muffin tin with 10 large paper cases.

3   Place butter, sugar, golden syrup, treacle and ground ginger in a saucepan over a gentle heat and stir until melted. Remove from the heat and stir in the milk, then beat in the egg. Fold in the flour. Spoon into the cases and bake for about 20 minutes until risen and firm to touch.

4   Whip the cream in a bowl until it is holding soft peaks. Stir in 2 tbsp of lemon curd.

5   Slice the top off each cake and set the tops aside. Cut a 2cm (¾in) hole in the middle of each cake and discard the little pieces. Spoon 1 tbsp of lemon curd into each hole and spread over the middle of the cakes. Replace the tops and pipe the lemon-cream mixture over the top.

6   Decorate with a small sprinkle of grated lemon rind and then serve.

Orange custard cupcakes

A true comfort food. Makes 10.

Ingredients

110g (4½oz) unsalted butter, softened
110g (4½oz) caster sugar
2 eggs, beaten
1 tbsp orange juice
1 tsp finely grated orange rind
110g (4½oz) self-raising flour

Orange custard

9 tbsp orange juice
80ml (2¾fl oz) water
2 tbsp plain flour
100g (4oz) caster sugar
3 egg yolks

Decoration

Orange segments

1. Pre-heat the oven to 180°C (350°F/Gas 4), then line a muffin tin with 10 large paper cases.

2. Make the orange custard. Mix all of the custard ingredients in a large, heatproof bowl over a saucepan of simmering water. Stir the mixture constantly until it is hot to the touch and thick enough to coat the back of a wooden spoon. Remove from the heat and cool, stirring occasionally so that a skin doesn't form. When cool, cover and chill.

3. Cream butter and sugar together until pale and creamy. Gradually beat in the eggs, a little at a time, beating well after each addition. Add the orange juice and rind and mix well. Fold in flour, using a metal spoon.

4. Spoon mixture into the prepared cases and bake for 20 minutes until well risen and golden. Remove from oven and transfer to a wire rack to cool.

5. When cool, remove the cases and slice the cupcakes in half horizontally. Spread the bottom half of each cupcake with the orange custard and replace the cupcake tops. Spoon the remaining custard on top of the cupcakes and decorate with the orange segments. Serve straightaway.

Passionfruit cream cakes

I adore passion fruit, and these cakes taste simply divine. Makes 10.

Ingredients

110g (4½oz) unsalted butter, softened
110g (4½oz) caster sugar
2 eggs, beaten
½ tsp vanilla essence
110g (4½oz) self-raising flour
A little milk

Passion-fruit cream

5 passion fruits
140g (5½oz) mascarpone
4 tbsp icing sugar

Decoration

2 passion fruits
Icing sugar for dusting

1   Pre-heat the oven to 180°C (350°F/Gas 4), then line a muffin tin with 10 large paper cases.

2   Cream the butter and sugar together until pale and creamy. Gradually beat in the eggs, a little at a time, beating well after each addition. Add the vanilla essence, mixing well. Fold in the flour, using a metal spoon. If the mixture is a little stiff, add a couple of spoonfuls of milk to create a better dropping consistency.

3   Spoon mixture into the cases and bake for 20 minutes until well risen and golden. Remove from the oven. Transfer to a wire rack to cool.

4   For the passion-fruit cream, halve the passion fruits and scoop out the seeds into a sieve placed over a bowl. Press with the back of a spoon to extract the juice. Put mascarpone, icing sugar and passion-fruit juice in a bowl and beat well.

5   To assemble, remove paper cases and slice the cakes horizontally into three. Bind the slices of cake together with passion-fruit cream. Top each cake with a little more passion-fruit cream. Halve the remaining passion fruits, scoop out the seeds, spoon them over the top of the cakes and then dust with icing sugar.

Peach Melba

A classic, and always popular, combination. Makes 10.

Ingredients
110g (4½oz) unsalted butter, softened
110g (4½oz) caster sugar
2 eggs, beaten
½ tsp vanilla essence
110g (4½oz) self-raising flour
A little milk

Good-quality vanilla ice cream
1 can peach halves, drained and sliced

Melba
225g (9oz) raspberries
30ml (2 tbsp) framboise liqueur
Icing sugar to taste

Filling
300ml (½pt) double cream

Decoration
Fresh raspberries

1   Pre-heat the oven to 180°C (350°F/Gas 4), then line a muffin tin with 10 large paper cases.

2   Make the Melba sauce. Put the raspberries and framboise liqueur in a food processor and whizz until it makes a sauce. Pass through a sieve to remove the pips and then add a little icing sugar to sweeten to taste.

3   Cream the butter and sugar together until pale and creamy. Gradually beat in the eggs, a little at a time, beating well after each addition. Add the vanilla essence, mixing well. Fold in the flour, using a metal spoon. If the mixture is a little stiff, add a couple of spoonfuls of milk to create a better dropping consistency.

4   Spoon mixture into the cases and bake for 20 minutes until well risen and golden. Remove from oven and transfer to a wire rack to cool. When cool, remove the cases and slice the cupcakes in half horizontally.

5   Whip the double cream in a clean bowl until it is holding gentle peaks.

6   Place a scoop of vanilla ice cream on the bottom half of each cupcake. Replace the top and lightly press down. Spoon the whipped cream over the top and place peach slices on top. Spoon over the Melba sauce and, lastly, decorate with a single raspberry on the top.

Strawberry fool

Perfect in the summer, when strawberries are in season. Makes 10.

Ingredients

110g (4½oz) unsalted butter, softened
110g (4½oz) caster sugar
2 eggs, beaten
½ tsp vanilla essence
110g (4½oz) self-raising flour
A little milk

Strawberry fool

450g (1lb) strawberries, topped
and tailed
125g (5oz) caster sugar
160ml (¼pt) custard
150ml (¼pt) double cream, whipped

Decoration

Fresh strawberries, sliced
Icing sugar

1   Pre-heat the oven to 180°C (350°F/Gas 4), then line a muffin tin with 10 large paper cases.

2   Make the fool. Put the strawberries and sugar in a food processor and whizz to make a purée. In a bowl, beat the custard into the strawberry purée and finally fold in the whipped double cream. Chill until needed.

3   Cream the butter and sugar together until pale and creamy. Gradually beat in the eggs, a little at a time, beating well after each addition. Add the vanilla essence, mixing well. Fold in the flour, using a metal spoon. If the mixture is a little stiff, add a couple of spoonfuls of milk to create a better dropping consistency.

4   Spoon this mixture into the prepared cases and bake for 20 minutes until well risen and golden. Remove from the oven and transfer to a wire rack to cool. When cool, remove the cases and slice the cupcakes in half horizontally. Spread the bottom half of each cupcake with the strawberry fool and replace the cupcake tops. Pipe the remaining fool over the top of the cupcakes. Decorate with the sliced strawberries and dust with icing sugar. Serve straightaway.

Tiramisu cupcakes

The sharp, coffee taste makes this cupcake a really adult dessert. Makes 10.

Ingredients

110g (4½oz) unsalted butter, softened
110g (4½oz) caster sugar
2 eggs, beaten
½ tsp vanilla essence
110g (4½oz) self-raising flour
A little milk

Mascarpone cream
250g (10oz) mascarpone
50g (2oz) icing sugar
180ml (6¼fl oz) double cream, whipped

Coffee mix
1 tbsp instant coffee
50ml (2fl oz) boiling water
4 tbsp Kahlua or another coffee-flavoured liqueur

Decoration
Grated plain chocolate

1   Pre-heat the oven to 180°C (350°F/Gas 4), then line a muffin tin with 10 large paper cases.

2   Cream the butter and sugar together until pale and creamy. Gradually beat in the eggs, a little at a time, beating well after each addition. Add the vanilla essence, mixing well. Fold in the flour, using a metal spoon. If the mixture is a little stiff, add a couple of spoonfuls of milk to create a better dropping consistency.

3   Spoon this mixture into the prepared cases and bake for 15–20 minutes until well risen and golden. Remove from the oven and transfer to a wire rack to cool.

4   To make the mascarpone cream, put the mascarpone, icing sugar and double cream in a bowl and whip well.

5   To make the coffee mix, dissolve the instant coffee in the boiling water and, when cool, add the liqueur.

6   Remove the paper cases and slice the cakes horizontally into three. Brush the cut sides of the cakes with the coffee mix. Reassemble the cakes, binding the slices together with mascarpone cream. Finally, top each cake with mascarpone cream and sprinkle with grated chocolate.

7   Refrigerate for several hours and then serve.

Victoria cupcakes

These are a great variation on the classic recipe. Makes 10.

Ingredients

110g (4½oz) unsalted butter, softened
110g (4½oz) caster sugar
2 eggs, beaten
½ tsp vanilla essence
110g (4½oz) self-raising flour
A little milk

Filling

Strawberry jam
160ml (½pt) double cream, whipped

Decoration

Icing sugar

1   Pre-heat the oven to 180°C (350°F/Gas 4), then line a muffin tin with 10 large paper cases.

2   Cream the butter and sugar together until pale and creamy. Gradually beat in the eggs, a little at a time, beating well after each addition. Add the vanilla essence, mixing well. Fold in the flour, using a metal spoon. If the mixture is a little stiff, add a couple of spoonfuls of milk to create a better dropping consistency.

3   Spoon this mixture into the prepared cases and bake for 20 minutes until well risen and golden. Remove from the oven and transfer to a wire rack to cool. When cool, remove the cases.

4   Slice the cupcakes into three slices horizontally. Spread these slices with alternate layers of jam and cream and sandwich together. Dust the tops with icing sugar.

Chocolate cupcakes

Chocolate & hazelnut cupcakes

Simply delicious. Makes 12.

Ingredients

100g (4oz) dark-chocolate pieces
100g (4oz) unsalted butter
100g (4oz) caster sugar
2 eggs, beaten
75g (3oz) self-raising flour
15g (½oz) cocoa powder
50g (2oz) hazelnuts, chopped

Topping

150ml (¼pint) double cream

Decoration

Toasted chopped hazelnuts
Grated chocolate

1 Pre-heat the oven to 180°C (350°F/Gas 4), then line a 12-hole bun tin with paper cases.

2 Put the chocolate pieces in a heatproof bowl, place this over a pan of simmering water and stir until melted. Allow to cool slightly. Cream the butter and sugar together until pale and creamy. Gradually beat in the eggs, a little at a time, beating well after each addition. Gently add the melted chocolate to the cake mixture. Fold in the flour and cocoa powder, using a metal spoon. Finally, add the chopped hazelnuts.

3 Spoon this mixture into the prepared cases and bake for 15–20 minutes until well risen and firm to the touch. Remove from the oven and transfer to a wire rack to cool.

4 Whip the cream until stiff and then spoon on to the cupcakes. Sprinkle with the toasted hazelnuts and grated chocolate.

Chocolate nutty caramel crispy cakes

These will be sure to satisfy any sweet tooth. Makes 12.

Ingredients

75g (3oz) milk chocolate, in pieces
50g (2oz) golden syrup
100g (4oz) butter
2 x chewy nut & caramel bars, chopped
50g (2oz) cornflakes

Topping

200g (8oz) milk chocolate, in pieces

Decoration

1 Snickers bar, sliced into 12 pieces

1   Line a 12-hole bun tin with paper cases.

2   Put the chocolate, syrup, butter and bars into a heavy-based saucepan over a very low heat and stir until melted

3   Fold in the cornflakes and mix well. Now divide this mixture between the paper cases.

4   For the topping, put the milk-chocolate pieces into a heatproof bowl, place this over a pan of simmering water and stir until melted. Spread the chocolate over the cakes and top with a slice of caramel bar. Chill until set.

Chocolate & strawberry topped cupcakes

Fresh strawberries really make these special cupcakes. Makes 12.

Ingredients

100g (4oz) unsalted butter
100g (4oz) caster sugar
2 eggs, beaten
½ tsp vanilla essence
100g (4oz) self-raising flour

Topping

150g (6oz) white chocolate, chopped
150g (6oz) cream cheese
6 tbsp crème fraîche
½ tsp vanilla essence
6 tbsp icing sugar, sifted

Decoration

Strawberries, halved
Plain chocolate (a couple of squares), melted

1 Pre-heat the oven to 180°C (350°F/Gas 4), then line a 12-hole bun tin with paper cases.

2 Cream butter and sugar together until pale and creamy. Gradually beat in the eggs, a little at a time, beating well after each addition. Add the vanilla essence. Fold in the flour, using a metal spoon.

3 Spoon this mixture into the prepared cases and bake for 15–20 minutes until well risen and firm to the touch. Remove from the oven and transfer to a wire rack to cool.

4 Melt the white chocolate in a heatproof bowl over a pan of simmering water; leave to cool for a few minutes. Beat the cream cheese, crème fraîche, vanilla essence and icing sugar together in a bowl. Stir in the cooled chocolate.

5 Spread this over the cupcakes, decorate with the strawberries and drizzle the melted plain chocolate over the top.

Chocolate brownie cupcakes

These are really moist and an all-time favourite. Makes 12.

Ingredients

75g (3oz) plain chocolate, chopped
75g (3oz) unsalted butter
1 egg
75g (3oz) caster sugar
½ tsp vanilla essence

Pinch of salt
25g (1oz) self-raising flour, sifted
50g (2oz) chopped mixed nuts

Decoration

Icing sugar

1   Pre-heat the oven to 180°C (350°F/Gas 4), then line a 12-hole bun tin with paper cases.

2   Place the chocolate and butter in a heatproof bowl over a pan of simmering water. Stir until melted. Then remove from the heat and cool slightly.

3   Beat in the egg, and then stir in the sugar, vanilla essence and pinch of salt. Fold the sifted flour into the mixture, and finally mix in the nuts.

4   Divide the mixture between the cases and bake for approximately 20 minutes, until the tops are just firm to the touch. Transfer to a wire rack and cool. Dust with icing sugar.

Chocolate chip cupcakes

Melt-in-the-mouth cupcakes, with a little crunch from the chocolate chips. Makes 12.

Ingredients

3 tbsp golden syrup
100g (4oz) demerara sugar
100g (4oz) butter
200g (8oz) self-raising flour

25g (1oz) cocoa powder
1 egg, beaten
140ml (5fl oz) whole milk
50g (2oz) chocolate chips

1   Pre-heat the oven to 180°C (350°F/Gas 4), then line a 12-hole bun tin with paper cases.

2   Place the golden syrup, sugar and butter in a saucepan, then melt gently over a low heat. Sift the flour and cocoa into this mixture and mix well. Lastly, beat in the egg, milk and chocolate chips.

3   Spoon the mixture into the paper cases and cook for 15–20 minutes. To check that they are cooked through, insert a sharp knife into the tops of the cupcakes; if it comes out cleanish, then they are cooked. If not, return them to the oven for a further few minutes.

Chocolate lace cupcakes

The delicate topping makes these a really elegant choice. Makes 12.

Ingredients

100g (4oz) unsalted butter
100g (4oz) caster sugar
2 eggs, beaten
100g (4oz) self-raising flour
3 tbsp cocoa powder

Decoration

Laced-patterned stencil, such as paper doily
or piece of lace
Icing sugar

1 Pre-heat the oven to 180°C (350°F/Gas 4), then line a 12-hole bun tin with paper cases.

2 Cream butter and sugar together until pale and creamy. Gradually beat in the eggs, a little at a time, beating well after each addition. Fold in the flour, using a metal spoon. Mix cocoa powder in a small bowl with some water to make a paste; add to the sponge mixture and fold in.

3 Spoon this mixture into the prepared cases and bake for 15–20 minutes until well risen and firm to the touch. Remove from the oven and transfer to a wire rack to cool.

4 When cool, lay the lace-patterned stencil over the top of each cake in turn and sift over the icing sugar. Carefully remove the stencil each time.

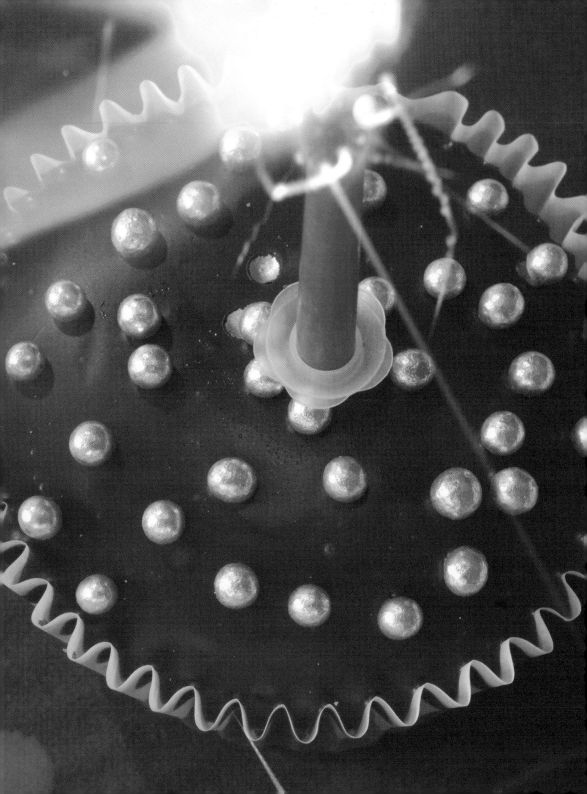

Sparkler cupcakes

These make a great impression when you want a dramatic centrepiece.
Makes 12.

Ingredients
125g (5oz) butter
125g (5oz) caster sugar
2 large eggs, beaten
125g (5oz) self-raising flour
3 level tbsp cocoa
4 tbsp milk

Topping
100g (4oz) dark chocolate, chopped
100ml (3½fl oz) double cream
Tiny edible silver balls
12 mini-sparklers

1 Pre-heat the oven to 200°C (400°F/Gas 6), then line a 12-hole bun tin with paper cases.

2 Cream the butter and sugar until pale and fluffy. Add the eggs, a little at a time, beating well after each addition. Using a metal spoon, fold in the flour and the cocoa. Add enough milk for a soft, dropping consistency. Alternatively, put all of the ingredients (apart from the milk) into a food processor, whizz until smooth and then add the milk.

3 Spoon the mixture into the paper cases and bake for 15–20 minutes, or until risen and firm on top. Transfer to a wire rack to cool.

4 To make the topping, put the chocolate in a heatproof bowl. Heat the cream in a saucepan until almost boiling and pour over the chocolate. Leave to stand for about 5 minutes and then stir until smooth. Leave the mixture to cool for 5–10 minutes before spreading over the cakes.

5 Sprinkle the cakes with the edible silver balls and insert a sparkler into the middle of each one. Light the sparklers just prior to serving.

White chocolate & coconut cupcakes

Perfect for an afternoon-tea spread. Makes 12.

Ingredients

100g (4oz) unsalted butter
100g (4oz) caster sugar
2 eggs, beaten
100g (4oz) self-raising flour
50g (2oz) white-chocolate buttons

Topping

75g (3oz) butter, softened
175g (7oz) icing sugar
50g (2oz) white-chocolate buttons, melted

Decoration

Desiccated coconut

1   Pre-heat the oven to 180°C (350°F/Gas 4), then line a 12-hole bun tin with paper cases.

2   Cream the butter and sugar together until pale and creamy. Gradually beat in the eggs, a little at a time, beating well after each addition. Fold in the flour, using a metal spoon. Finally, add the chocolate buttons and mix thoroughly.

3   Spoon this mixture into the prepared cases and bake for 15–20 minutes until well risen and firm to the touch. Remove from the oven and transfer to a wire rack to cool.

4   Beat the butter in a bowl until light and fluffy. Gradually add the icing sugar, stirring well. Lastly, mix in the melted white chocolate.

5   Top the cupcakes with the icing and then sprinkle the tops liberally with desiccated coconut.

Kids' cupcakes

Buzzy bee cupcakes

Get your children all a-buzz with these great cupcakes. Makes 12.

Ingredients

100g (4oz) butter
100g (4oz) caster sugar
2 eggs, beaten
100g (4oz) self-raising flour
2 tbsp milk

Icing

2 tbsp water
150g (6oz) icing sugar
Yellow food colouring

Decoration

Black-coloured writing icing
12 After Dinner mints

1   Pre-heat the oven to 200°C (400°F/Gas 6), then line a 12-hole bun tin with paper cases.

2   Cream the butter and sugar until pale and fluffy. Add the eggs, a little at a time, beating well after each addition. Using a metal spoon, fold in the flour. If the mixture is too dry, add a little milk for a soft, dropping consistency. Alternatively, put all of the ingredients (apart from the milk) into a food processor, whizz until smooth and then add the milk.

3   Spoon mixture into the paper cases and bake for 15–20 minutes, or until risen and firm on top. Transfer to a wire rack to cool.

4   For the icing, put the water in a bowl, sift in the icing sugar and slowly mix until smooth. Add a few drops of the yellow food colouring and mix well. Spoon this mixture on top of the cupcakes.

5   With the writing icing, create some black stripes over ¾ of the cupcake. Cut the After Dinner mints in half and place on top of the stripes to make the wings. Lastly, use the writing icing to create three little dots for the bee's head.

Butterfly cupcakes

Perfect for all of your little princesses. Makes 12.

Ingredients

100g (4oz) butter
100g (4oz) caster sugar
2 eggs, beaten
100g (4oz) self-raising flour
2 tbsp milk

Butter icing

75g (3oz) butter
175g (7oz) icing sugar
1–2 tbsp milk

Decoration

Small silver balls
Jelly laces
Icing sugar

1   Pre-heat the oven to 200°C (400°F/Gas 6), then line a 12-hole bun tin with paper cases.

2   Cream butter and sugar until pale and fluffy. Add the eggs, a little at a time, beating well after each addition. Using a metal spoon, fold in flour. If the mixture is too dry, add a little milk for a soft, dropping consistency. Alternatively, put all the ingredients (apart from the milk) into a food processor, whizz until smooth and then add the milk.

3   Spoon the mixture into the paper cases and bake for 15–20 minutes, or until risen and firm on the top. Transfer to a wire rack to cool.

4   To make the butter icing, cream the butter until soft and gradually add the icing sugar, beating well. Add a few drops of milk for the right consistency.

5   Slice the tops off the cupcakes and then cut each top in half. Spoon a dollop of butter icing on the top. Replace the tops to make the wings. Use the silver balls to decorate, with jelly laces for antennae.

6   Dust with icing sugar.

Croaky frog cupcakes

Kiss these, and who knows what you will get. Makes 12.

Ingredients

100g (4oz) butter
100g (4oz) caster sugar
2 eggs, beaten
100g (4oz) self-raising flour
2 tbsp milk

Icing

2 tbsp water
150g (6oz) icing sugar
Green food colouring

Decoration

Large marshmallows
Coloured writing icing

1   Pre-heat the oven to 200°C (400°F/Gas 6), then line a 12-hole bun tin with paper cases.

2   Cream butter and sugar until pale and fluffy. Add the eggs, a little at a time, beating well after each addition. Using a metal spoon, fold in the flour. If the mixture is too dry, add a little milk to make it a soft, dropping consistency. Alternatively, put all ingredients (apart from milk) into a food processor, whizz until smooth and add the milk.

3   Spoon the mixture into the paper cases and bake for 15–20 minutes, or until risen and firm on the top. Transfer to a wire rack to cool.

4   To make the icing, put the water into a bowl, gradually sift in the icing sugar and mix until smooth. Add a few drops of the green food colouring and mix well. Add more colouring for a stronger colour.

5   Spoon the icing over the cakes.

6   Place two marshmallows on their sides at the back of each cupcake for the frog's eyes. Use a dab of writing icing to make the pupils. Then use the writing icing to create a mouth and nose.

Frosted snowmen

These are great for the winter, but can be enjoyed at any time of year.
Makes 12.

Ingredients

100g (4oz) butter
100g (4oz) caster sugar
2 eggs, beaten
100g (4oz) self-raising flour
2 tbsp milk

Icing

1 egg white
175g (7oz) caster sugar

Pinch of salt
30ml (2 tbsp) water
Pinch of cream of tartar

Decoration

12 white marshmallows
Coloured writing icing
Red laces (sweets)
Small sweets to decorate

1. Pre-heat the oven to 200°C (400°F/Gas 6), then line a 12-hole bun tin with paper cases.

2. Cream the butter and sugar until pale and fluffy. Add the eggs, a bit at a time, beating well after each addition. Using a metal spoon, fold in the flour. If the mixture is too dry, add a little milk for a soft, dropping consistency. Alternatively, put all of the ingredients (apart from the milk) into a food processor, whizz until smooth and then add the milk.

3. Spoon the mixture into the paper cases and bake for 15–20 minutes, or until risen and firm on top. Transfer to a wire rack to cool.

4. To make the icing, place all of the ingredients into a heatproof bowl and whisk lightly. Place the bowl over a pan of hot water and whisk for about 6 minutes, until the mixture thickens and can hold peaks.

5. Take the cakes out of their cases and cover them in the icing.

6. Decorate the cakes. Place a white marshmallow on top of each as the snowman's head and use the writing icing to make eyes and a mouth. The laces can be used as scarves and the other sweets could be used to make buttons. Use the writing icing to draw arms.

Pink piggy cupcakes

Don't be put off by the name – kids love these cupcakes. Makes 12.

Ingredients

100g (4oz) butter
100g (4oz) caster sugar
2 eggs, beaten
100g (4oz) self-raising flour
2 tbsp milk

Icing

2 tbsp water
150g (6oz) icing sugar
Pink food colouring

Decoration

Marshmallows
Black-coloured writing icing
12 After Dinner mints
Currants
Ready-rolled icing

1   Pre-heat the oven to 200°C (400°F/Gas 6), then line a 12-hole bun tin with paper cases.

2   Cream butter and sugar until pale and fluffy. Add eggs, a little at a time, beating well after each addition. Using a metal spoon, fold in flour. If the mixture is too dry, add a little milk for a soft, dropping consistency. Alternatively, put all the ingredients (apart from the milk) into a food processor, whizz until smooth and then add milk.

3   Spoon the mixture into the paper cases and bake for 15–20 minutes, or until risen and firm on top. Transfer to a wire rack to cool.

4   For the icing, put the water into a bowl, gradually sift in icing sugar and mix until smooth. Add a few drops of pink food colouring and mix well. Add a few more drops of colouring for a stronger colour. Mix well.

5   Spoon this mixture on top of the cupcakes.

6   Place a marshmallow on each cake for the pig's nose. Use black writing icing to make two dots on top of the nose. Two currants will make the pig's eyes. For the ears, add a few drops of food colouring to a piece of the ready-rolled icing, break into small pieces and mould into the shape of an ear. Place two on top of each cupcake.

Smiley face cupcakes

These will bring a smile to any child's face. Makes 12.

Ingredients

100g (4oz) butter
100g (4oz) caster sugar
2 eggs, beaten
100g (4oz) self-raising flour
2 tbsp milk

Icing

2 tbsp water
150g (6oz) icing sugar
Food colouring of your choice

Decoration

Coloured writing icing
Small sweets, Smarties, jelly tots,
chocolate buttons etc.

1 Pre-heat the oven to 200°C (400°F/Gas 6), then line a 12-hole bun tin with paper cases.

2 Cream butter and sugar until pale and fluffy. Add eggs, a little at a time, beating well after each addition. Using a metal spoon, fold in the flour. If the mixture is too dry, add a little milk for a soft, dropping consistency. Alternatively, put all the ingredients (apart from the milk) into a food processor, whizz until smooth and then add milk.

3 Spoon the mixture into the paper cases and bake for 15–20 minutes, or until risen and firm on top. Transfer to a wire rack to cool.

4 To make the icing, put the water in a bowl, gradually sift in the icing sugar and mix until smooth. Add a few drops of the food colouring of your choice.

5 Spoon this mixture on top of the cupcakes.

6 Decorate the cakes, using the writing icing and sweets to create your choice of smiley face. Smarties for the eyes, a line of jelly tots for the mouth . . . the choice is yours.

Sprinkle cupcakes

These cupcakes are simplicity itself.
Makes 12.

Ingredients

100g (4oz) butter
100g (4oz) caster sugar
2 eggs, beaten
100g (4oz) self-raising flour
2 tbsp milk

Butter icing

75g (3oz) butter
175g (7oz) icing sugar
1–2 tbsp milk

Decoration

Hundreds and thousands

1   Pre-heat the oven to 200°C (400°F/Gas 6), then line a 12-hole bun tin with paper cases.

2   Cream the butter and sugar until pale and fluffy. Add the egg, a little at a time, beating well after each addition. Using a metal spoon, fold in the flour. If the mixture is too dry, add a little milk for a soft, dropping consistency. Alternatively, put all of the ingredients (apart from the milk) into a food processor, whizz until smooth and then add the milk.

3   Spoon the mixture into the paper cases and bake for 15–20 minutes, or until risen and firm on top. Transfer to a wire rack to cool.

4   For the butter icing, cream the butter until soft, and then gradually add the icing sugar, beating well. Add a few drops of milk for the right consistency.

5   Top the cupcakes with the icing and then liberally sprinkle them with the hundreds and thousands.

Toffee & marshmallow crispie cakes

Bake these, then just stand back and watch them go. Makes 12.

Ingredients

125g (5oz) toffees
125g (5oz) unsalted butter

125g (5oz) marshmallows
125g (5oz) Rice Krispies

1   Line a 12-hole bun tray with paper cases.

2   Put the toffees, butter and marshmallows into a large, heavy-based pan. Over a low heat, gently melt them, stirring all the time. When everything has melted, remove from the heat and stir in the Rice Krispies.

3   Spoon the mixture into the prepared cases and leave it to set.

Liqueur cupcakes

Amaretto cupcakes

A touch of this Italian liqueur transforms these cupcakes into
something special. Makes 12.

Ingredients

100g (4oz) unsalted butter
100g (4oz) caster sugar
2 eggs, beaten
100g (4oz) self-raising flour
50g (2oz) sultanas
60ml (4 tbsp) amaretto liqueur

Topping

284ml (½pt) double cream
50g (2oz) icing sugar
3 tbsp amaretto liqueur
50g (2oz) amaretti biscuits, crushed

Decoration

Amaretti biscuits, crushed

1 Pre-heat the oven to 180°C (350°F/Gas 4), then line a 12-hole bun tin with paper cases.

2 Cream the butter and sugar together until pale and creamy.
Gradually beat in the eggs, a little at a time, beating well after each addition. Fold in the flour, using a metal spoon. Finally, combine with the sultanas.

3 Spoon this mixture into the prepared cases and bake for 15–20 minutes until well risen and golden. Remove from the oven and transfer to a wire rack to cool.

4 When cool, pierce the tops of the cupcakes with a fork and spoon over the amaretto.

5 To make the topping, whip the cream, icing sugar and amaretto together until thick, then fold in the crushed amaretti biscuits. Use this to ice the cupcakes, then sprinkle them with a little more of the crushed amaretti biscuits.

Apple & Calvados cupcakes

These are really moist and succulent cupcakes, perfect with a dollop of cream.
Makes 12.

Ingredients

100g (4oz) apple, grated
15ml (1 tbsp) Calvados
100g (4oz) unsalted butter
100g (4oz) caster sugar
2 eggs, beaten
100g (4oz) self-raising flour
1 tsp cinnamon

Caramelised apple

70g (3oz) butter
4 apples, peeled, cored and sliced
4 tbsp sugar

Caramel sauce

75g (3oz) butter
50g (2oz) soft brown sugar
225g (9oz) icing sugar
1 tbsp milk

1   Pre-heat the oven to 180°C (350°F/Gas 4), then line a 12-hole bun tin with paper cases.

2   In a small bowl, mix the grated apple and Calvados. Cream the butter and sugar together until pale and creamy. Gradually beat in the eggs, a little at a time, beating well after each addition. Fold in the flour and cinnamon, using a metal spoon. Add the apple-and-calvados mixture.

3   Spoon this mixture into the prepared cases and bake for 15–20 minutes until well risen and golden. Remove from the oven and transfer to a wire rack to cool.

4   In a large pan, melt the butter and then fry the sliced apples until golden. Remove from the heat and sprinkle with sugar. Lay the sliced apples on top of the cooled cupcakes.

5   To make the sauce, melt the butter in a heavy saucepan over a low heat. Add the brown sugar and stir until the sugar has melted and turned a light-golden colour. Remove from the heat and add the icing sugar and milk, mixing well. Pour about 1 tablespoon of the sauce over each cupcake.

Baileys & chocolate chip cupcakes

Perfect for a winter dinner party. Makes 12.

Ingredients

100g (4oz) unsalted butter
100g (4oz) caster sugar
2 eggs, beaten
100g (4oz) self-raising flour
50g (2oz) chocolate chips
60ml (4 tbsp) Baileys liqueur

Baileys icing

284ml (½pt) double cream
50g (2oz) icing sugar
3 tbsp Baileys liqueur

Decoration

Chocolate chips

1   Pre-heat the oven to 180°C (350°F/Gas 4), then line a 12-hole bun tin with paper cases.

2   Cream the butter and sugar together until pale and creamy. Gradually beat in the eggs, a little at a time, beating well after each addition. Fold in the flour, using a metal spoon. Finally, mix in the chocolate chips.

3   Spoon this mixture into the prepared cases and bake for 15–20 minutes until well risen and golden. Remove from the oven and transfer to a wire rack to cool. When cool, pierce the tops of the cupcakes with a fork and pour over the Baileys.

4   For the icing, combine all of the ingredients in a bowl and whisk until stiff, but don't overwhip.

5   Ice the cooled cupcakes with the Baileys icing and finally decorate with the chocolate chips.

Champagne cupcakes

Truly indulgent cupcakes, which are well worth the expense. Makes 10.

Ingredients

125g (5oz) plain flour
1 tsp baking powder
125g (5oz) caster sugar
A small pinch of salt

60ml (2fl oz) champagne
60ml (2fl oz) sunflower oil
2 eggs, separated
75g (3oz) raisins

1 Preheat the oven to 180°C (350°F/Gas 4). Line a bun tray with 10 gold paper cases.

2 Mix the flour, baking powder, sugar and salt in a bowl. Gradually add the champagne and oil, mixing well. Then add the egg yolks, beating well after each addition.

3 Whisk the egg whites until stiff and then gently fold into the batter with a metal spoon. Gently fold in the raisins.

4 Spoon the mixture into the cases and bake for about 20 minutes. Remove from the oven and cool on a wire rack.

Cherry & brandy cupcakes

Cherries and brandy make a classic combination. Makes 12.

Ingredients

100g (4oz) unsalted butter
100g (4oz) caster sugar
2 eggs, beaten
100g (4oz) self-raising flour
50g (2oz) glacé cherries
60ml (2fl oz) brandy

Brandy icing

284ml (½pt) double cream
50g (2oz) icing sugar
3 tbsp brandy

Decoration

12 cherry-and-liqueur-filled chocolates

1 Pre-heat the oven to 180°C (350°F/Gas 4), then line a 12-hole bun tin with paper cases.

2 Cream the butter and sugar together until pale and creamy. Gradually beat in the eggs, a little at a time, beating well after each addition. Fold in the flour, using a metal spoon. Finally, mix in the cherries.

3 Spoon this mixture into the prepared cases and bake for 15–20 minutes until well risen and golden. Remove from the oven and transfer to a wire rack to cool. When cool, pierce the tops of the cupcakes with a fork and pour over the brandy.

4 For the icing, combine all of the ingredients in a bowl and whisk until stiff, but don't overwhip.

5 Ice the cooled cupcakes with the brandy icing and decorate each with a cherry-and-liqueur chocolate.

Grand Marnier & summer berry mousse cupcakes

These make a spectacular summer dessert. Makes 12.

Ingredients

4 eggs
125g (5oz) caster sugar
125g (5oz) plain flour
40 g (1½oz) butter, melted
60ml (2fl oz) Grand Marnier

Mousse

20ml (4 tsp) powdered gelatine
75g (3oz) caster sugar
500g (1lb 2oz) mixed berries (straw-berries, raspberries, blackcurrants etc.)
15ml (1 tbsp) lemon juice
350ml (12fl oz) double cream

Decoration

Mixed berries
Icing sugar

1 Pre-heat the oven to 180°C (350°F/Gas 4), then line a 12-hole bun tin with paper cases.

2 Whisk the eggs and sugar together in a large, heatproof bowl over a pan of hot water until the mixture is pale and thick. Remove from the pan and whisk until cool.

3 Sift half the flour into the mixture and lightly fold in with a metal spoon. Pour in melted butter around the edge of the bowl and then sift in the remaining flour. Fold gently until combined. Spoon a little mixture into the cases so that the bottom is covered with mixture.

4 Bake for 10–15 minutes until firm, then leave to cool on a wire rack.

5 Sprinkle the gelatine over 3 tbsp water; leave to soften. Dissolve the sugar in 50ml (2fl oz) water in a saucepan. Bring to the boil, then remove from the heat. Stir in the gelatine until dissolved.

6 Put the gelatine mixture into a food processor, add the berries and lemon juice and whizz until smooth. Leave until it starts to thicken (it shouldn't set).

7 Pierce the tops of the cakes with a fork and pour over the Grand Marnier. Whip the cream until thickened and then mix with the berry mixture. Spoon this mixture over the tops of the cupcakes. Chill until set. When set, remove the paper cases, decorate with the mixed berries and icing sugar and serve with cream.

Lemoncello cupcakes

Lemoncello is a classic Italian liqueur that makes a really zesty dessert.
Makes 12.

Ingredients

100g (4oz) unsalted butter
100g (4oz) caster sugar
2 eggs, beaten
100g (4oz) self-raising flour
Finely grated rind of 1 lemon
60ml (2fl oz) lemoncello

Topping

284ml (½pt) double cream
50g (2oz) icing sugar
3 tbsp lemoncello

Decoration

Finely grated lemon rind

1   Pre-heat the oven to 180°C (350°F/Gas 4), then line a 12-hole bun tin with paper cases.

2   Cream the butter and sugar together until pale and creamy.
Gradually beat in the eggs, a little at a time, beating well after each addition.
Fold in the flour, using a metal spoon. Finally, stir in the grated lemon rind.

3   Spoon this mixture into the prepared cases and bake for 15–20 minutes until well risen and golden. Remove from the oven and transfer to a wire rack to cool.

4   When cool, pierce the tops of the cupcakes with a fork and spoon over the lemoncello.

5   To make the topping, whip the cream, icing sugar and lemoncello together until thick.

6   Use this to ice the cupcakes, then sprinkle them with a little more of the grated lemon rind.

Rum-laced cupcakes

The rum in these delicious cupcakes adds a really intense flavour. Makes 12.

Ingredients

175g (7oz) unsalted butter, softened
175g (7oz) caster sugar
3 large eggs
175g (7oz) self-raising flour

Decoration

300ml (½pt) double cream, whipped
25g (1oz) icing sugar, sifted
3 tbsp rum
50g (2oz) plain chocolate, grated

1   Pre-heat the oven to 180°C (350°F/Gas 4), then line a 12-hole bun tin with paper cases.

2   Place the butter, caster sugar, eggs and flour in a food processor and whizz until smooth.

3   Spoon the mixture into the paper cases and cook for 15–20 minutes until well risen and golden on top. Place on a wire rack to cool.

4   To make the topping, mix the whipped double cream, icing sugar and rum together. When the cakes are cool, spread the mixture over the cakes. Finally, sprinkle with the grated chocolate.

Cupcakes for special diets

Dairy-free cherry cupcakes

Makes 12.

Ingredients

180g (7½oz) self-raising flour, sifted
150g (6oz) soft brown sugar
Pinch salt
50g (2oz) glacé cherries, chopped
240ml (8fl oz) water

30ml (2 tbsp) vegetable oil
1 tbsp vinegar
2 tsp vanilla essence

Decoration

Icing sugar

1 Pre-heat the oven to 180°C (350°F/Gas 4), then line a 12-hole bun tin with paper cases.

2 In a large bowl, mix all of the dry ingredients together. Then add the chopped glacé cherries and stir. Make a well in the centre and pour in the wet ingredients. Beat well with a wooden spoon until smooth.

3 Spoon the mixture into the prepared paper cases. Bake in the oven for 20 minutes until golden and firm to the touch. Transfer to a wire rack to cool. Decorate by sprinkling icing sugar over the top.

Dairy-free sultana cupcakes

Makes 12.

Ingredients

180g (7½oz) self-raising flour, sifted
150g (6oz) soft brown sugar
Pinch salt
50g (2oz) sultanas

240ml (8fl oz) water
30ml (2 tbsp) vegetable oil
1 tbsp vinegar
1 tsp vanilla essence

1 Pre-heat the oven to 180°C (350°F/Gas 4), then line a 12-hole bun tin with paper cases.

2 In a large bowl, mix all of the dry ingredients together. Then add the sultanas and stir.

3 Make a well in the centre and pour in the wet ingredients. Beat well with a wooden spoon until smooth.

4 Spoon the mixture into the prepared paper cases. Bake in the oven for 20 minutes until golden and firm to the touch. Transfer to a wire rack to cool.

Low-sugar carrot cupcakes

Makes 12.

Ingredients

240g (9½oz) carrots, coarsely grated
2 eggs
100ml (3½fl oz) vegetable oil
Grated rind and juice of 1 orange
125g (5oz) caster sugar
225g (9oz) self-raising flour
½ tsp bicarbonate of soda
½ tsp baking powder
50g (2oz) ready-to-eat apricots,
  roughly chopped

Topping

200g (8oz) pack extra-light cream cheese
1 tbsp orange curd
1 tbsp hazelnuts, toasted and chopped

1   Pre-heat the oven to 180°C (350°F/Gas 4), then line a 12-hole bun tin with paper cases.

2   Place the carrots in a sieve and squeeze out any excess juice.

3   Beat together the eggs, oil, orange rind, orange juice and sugar. Sieve in the flour, bicarbonate of soda and baking powder and beat well.

4   Using a metal spoon, fold in the carrots and apricots.

5   Spoon the mixture into the prepared cases and bake for 20–25 minutes, until firm to the touch. Test with a skewer to ensure that the cupcakes are cooked through. Transfer to a wire rack to cool.

6   For the topping, beat together the cream cheese and orange curd. Smooth over the top of the cupcakes and finally sprinkle with the toasted hazelnuts.

Sugar-free fruitcake cupcakes

Makes 12.

Ingredients

550g (1¼lb) plain flour, sifted
½ tsp bicarbonate of soda
1 tsp mixed spice
1 tsp ground nutmeg
225g (9oz) unsalted butter

330g (13oz) raisins
220g (8½oz) sultanas
110g (4½oz) mixed peel
280ml (½pt) beer
3 eggs

1 Pre-heat the oven to 170°C (325°F/Gas 5), then line a 12-hole bun tin with paper cases.

2 In a large bowl, sift in the flour, bicarbonate of soda, mixed spice and nutmeg. Cut the butter into small chunks and rub into the flour mixture using your fingertips, until you achieve a breadcrumb consistency.

3 Add all of the fruit to the flour mix and stir well. Make a well in the centre. Whisk the beer and eggs in a separate bowl until frothy and pour into the well in the flour mixture. Beat well.

4 Spoon the mixture into the prepared cases and bake for 25–30 minutes, until firm to the touch. Test with a skewer to ensure that the cupcakes are cooked through.

Eggless fruitcake cupcakes

Makes 12.

Ingredients

200g (8oz) butter
200g (8oz) soft brown sugar
200g (8oz) sultanas
200g (8oz) raisins
100g (4oz) glacé cherries, chopped

125g (5oz) chopped mixed nuts
150ml (¼pt) warm water
1 tsp bicarbonate of soda
A little warm water
400g (14oz) plain flour
1 tsp mixed spice
½ tsp ground cinnamon

1   Pre-heat the oven to 180°C (350°F/Gas 4), then line a 12-hole bun tin with paper cases.

2   Put the butter, brown sugar, sultanas, raisins, cherries and nuts into a large saucepan with 150ml (¼pt) warm water. Place over a gentle heat and slowly bring to the boil, stirring continually. Boil gently for 5 minutes. Remove from the heat and allow to cool.

3   Dissolve the bicarbonate of soda in a little warm water and add to the fruit mixture. Stir well. Sift in the flour and spices and beat well.

4   Spoon the mixture into the prepared paper cases.

5   Bake in the oven for 15–20 minutes until golden and firm to the touch. Transfer to a wire rack to cool.

Eggless vanilla cupcakes

Makes 12.

Ingredients

225g (9oz) self-raising flour
2 tsp baking powder
180g (7½oz) caster sugar
6 tbsp vegetable oil

240ml (8fl oz) water
1½ tsp vanilla essence

Decoration

Icing sugar, sifted

1 Pre-heat the oven to 180°C (350°F/Gas 4), then line a 12-hole bun tin with paper cases.

2 Sift the flour and baking powder into a large mixing bowl. Then stir in the caster sugar. Make a well in the bottom. Add the oil, water and vanilla essence and mix well.

3 Spoon the mixture into the prepared paper cases.

4 Bake in the oven for 20–25 minutes until firm to the touch.
Transfer to a wire rack to cool. Dust with icing sugar to serve.

Gluten-free blueberry cupcakes

Makes 12.

Ingredients

180g (7½oz) rice flour
45g (2oz) tapioca flour
1 tsp bicarbonate of soda
2 tsp gluten-free baking powder
145g (5½oz) caster sugar
60g (2½oz) butter, melted and cooled

1 egg, beaten
60g (2½oz) buttermilk
160g (6½oz) blueberries

Decoration

Icing sugar

1   Pre-heat the oven to 180°C (350°F/Gas 4), then line a 12-hole bun tin with paper cases.

2   Sift the flours, bicarbonate of soda and baking powder into a large bowl. Add the sugar and mix well. Make a well in the centre of the mix.

3   Whisk together the cooled butter, egg and buttermilk in another bowl. Pour this mixture into the well of the dry ingredients and stir gently. Finally, stir in the blueberries.

4   Spoon the mixture into the prepared cases and bake for 20–25 minutes until firm to the touch.

5   Dust with icing sugar prior to serving.

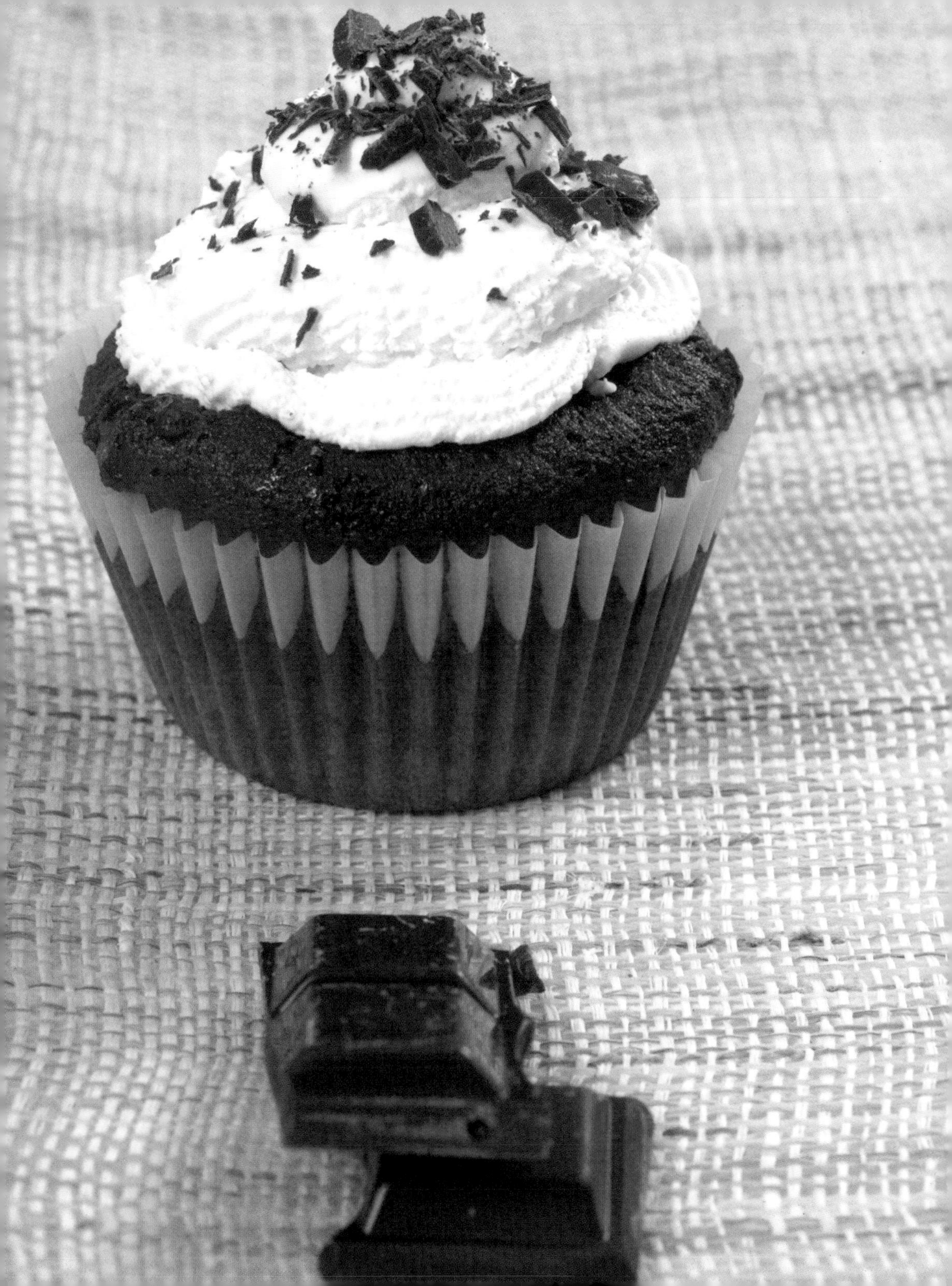

Gluten-free chocolate brownie cupcakes

Makes 12.

Ingredients

50g (2oz) good-quality, gluten-free plain chocolate
100g (4oz) butter
200g (8oz) caster sugar
2 eggs, lightly whisked
1 tsp vanilla essence

80g (3oz) ground almonds
2 tsp gluten-free baking powder
100g (4oz) chopped nuts

Decoration

Icing sugar

1 Pre-heat the oven to 180°C (350°F/Gas 4), then line a 12-hole bun tin with paper cases.

2 Break the chocolate into pieces and place in a heatproof bowl over a pan of gently simmering water. Stir until the chocolate has melted. Set aside.

3 Cream the butter and sugar until pale and fluffy, then gradually beat in the eggs, a little at a time. Stir in the vanilla essence and melted chocolate. Lastly, stir in the ground almonds, gluten-free baking powder and chopped nuts.

4 Spoon the mixture into the prepared cases and bake for 20–25 minutes until firm to the touch.

5 Dust with icing sugar prior to serving.

Celebration cupcakes

Happy birthday cupcakes

These are a great alternative to the traditional large birthday cake. Makes 12.

Ingredients

100g (4oz) unsalted butter
100g (4oz) caster sugar
2 eggs, beaten
100g (4oz) self-raising flour
½ tsp vanilla essence

Topping

185g (7½oz) icing sugar, sifted
1 egg white
¾ tsp lemon juice
Food colouring of your choice

Decoration

Candle
Sweets

1 Pre-heat the oven to 180°C (350°F/Gas 4), then line a 12-hole bun tin with paper cases.

2 Cream the butter and sugar together until pale and creamy. Next, beat in the eggs, a little at a time, beating well after each addition. Fold in the flour, using a metal spoon. Stir in the vanilla essence.

3 Spoon this mixture into the prepared cases and bake for 15–20 minutes until well risen and golden. Remove from the oven and transfer to a wire rack to cool.

4 For the topping, gradually add the sifted icing sugar to the egg white, beating as you go until it is thick and glossy. Add the lemon juice and a few drops of food colouring to the mixture and beat. Decorate with the sweets.

Christmas snowflake cupcakes

Beautiful cupcakes for the festive season. Makes 12.

Ingredients

100g (4oz) unsalted butter
100g (4oz) caster sugar
2 eggs, beaten
100g (4oz) self-raising flour
50g (2oz) mincemeat from a jar
50g (2oz) glacé cherries, chopped
Finely grated rind of 1 orange
1 tsp mixed spice

Decoration

Ready-rolled white icing
Fluted cutter
Snowflake cutter
Silver edible glitter
Some apricot jam, warmed and strained
Small edible silver balls

1 Pre-heat the oven to 180°C (350°F/Gas 4), then line a 12-hole bun tin with paper cases.

2 Cream the butter and sugar together until pale and creamy. Gradually beat in the eggs, a little at a time, beating well after each addition. Fold in the flour, using a metal spoon. Finally, add the mincemeat, cherries, orange rind and mixed spice.

3 Spoon this mixture into the prepared cases and bake for 15–20 minutes until well risen and golden. Remove from the oven and transfer to a wire rack to cool.

4 To decorate, roll out the icing to the desired thickness, and, using the fluted cutter, cut out rounds large enough almost to cover the cakes. Then use the snowflake cutter to cut out 12 smaller snowflakes. Dust the snowflakes with the edible glitter.

5 Spread some warm, strained apricot jam on to the cakes and place a fluted round on top of each cake. Put a dab of jam in the middle of each round and place a snowflake on top. Decorate the edges of the icing with the silver balls.

Diwali cupcakes

Diwali, the Hindu Festival of Lights, is one of the most popular festivals in South Asia, and is celebrated by Jains and Sikhs, as well as Hindus. As part of it, many honour Lakshmi, the goddess of wealth, with small altars adorned with money and pictures. It is called the 'Festival of Lights' because houses, shops and public places are decorated with small oil lamps placed in rows.
Makes 12.

Ingredients

110g (4½oz) unsalted butter, softened
110g (4½oz) caster sugar
2 eggs, beaten
110g (4½oz) self-raising flour

Topping

2 tbsp water
145g (5½oz) icing sugar
White edible glitter

Decoration

Candles
Chocolate money

1 Pre-heat the oven to 180°C (350°F/Gas 4), then line a 12-hole bun tin with paper cases.

2 Cream the butter and sugar together until pale and creamy. Gradually beat in the eggs, a little at a time, beating well after each addition. Fold in the flour, using a metal spoon.

3 Spoon this mixture into the prepared cases and bake for 15–20 minutes until well risen and golden. Remove from the oven and transfer to a wire rack to cool.

4 To make the icing, put the water in a bowl and gradually sift in the icing sugar. Stir well. Spoon over the cakes and then dust with the edible glitter.

5 Decorate each cupcake with a candle and some chocolate money.

Easter-nest cupcakes

Add a few fluffy chicks for a splendid table centrepiece.
Makes 12.

Ingredients

100g (4oz) unsalted butter
100g (4oz) caster sugar
2 eggs, beaten
½ tsp vanilla essence
100g (4oz) self-raising flour

Chocolate butter icing

1 tbsp cocoa powder
2 tbsp boiling water

80g (3oz) unsalted butter, softened
180g (7½oz) icing sugar, sieved
15–30ml (1–2 tbsp) milk

Decoration

5 chocolate flake bars
Chocolate eggs

1   Pre-heat the oven to 180°C (350°F/Gas 4), then line a 12-hole bun tin with paper cases.

2   Cream the butter and sugar together until pale and creamy. Gradually beat in the eggs, a little at a time, beating well after each addition. Add the vanilla essence, mixing well. Now fold in the flour, using a metal spoon.

3   Spoon this mixture into the prepared cases and bake for 15–20 minutes until well risen and golden. Remove from the oven and transfer to a wire rack to cool.

4   To make the chocolate butter icing, mix the cocoa powder with the boiling water and leave to cool. Put the butter in a bowl and beat until soft and fluffy. Gradually add the icing sugar, milk and cooled cocoa mix. Beat well.

5   Spoon this mixture on to the cakes and spread it out. Make nests from the flake bars and place the chocolate eggs inside.

Eid al-Fitr cupcakes

The Muslim holy month of Ramadan concludes with the celebration of Eid al-Fitr, a time of celebration, goodwill and unity. Makes 12.

Ingredients

100g (4oz) unsalted butter
100g (4oz) caster sugar
2 eggs, beaten
2 tbsp runny honey
100g (4oz) self-raising flour
50g (2oz) dates, roughly chopped

Icing

2 tbsp water
150g (6oz) icing sugar
Blue food colouring

Decoration

Ready-rolled white icing
Edible silver balls

1 Pre-heat the oven to 180°C (350°F/Gas 4), then line a 12-hole bun tin with paper cases.

2 Cream the butter and sugar together until pale and creamy. Gradually beat in the eggs, a little at a time, beating well after each addition. Add the honey, stirring well. Fold in the flour, using a metal spoon. Finally, combine with the chopped dates.

3 Spoon this mixture into the prepared cases and bake for 15–20 minutes until well risen and golden. Remove from the oven and transfer to a wire rack to cool.

4 To make the icing, put the water in a bowl and sift in the icing sugar. Stir in enough of the food colouring to make a dark-blue colour.

5 Using the ready-rolled white icing, cut out a circle for the moon and some small star shapes. Place on top of the cupcakes. Place some small silver balls on top as well.

Halloween chocolate cobweb cupcakes

A few sweetie spiders will really finish off these cupcakes. Makes 12.

Ingredients

100g (4oz) unsalted butter
100g (4oz) caster sugar
2 eggs, beaten
100g (4oz) self-raising flour
3 tbsp cocoa powder

Ganache topping

150ml (¼pt) double cream
125g (5oz) plain chocolate, broken
into pieces

Decoration

50g (2oz) white chocolate
Spider sweets

1 Pre-heat the oven to 180°C (350°F/Gas 4), then line a 12-hole bun tin with paper cases.

2 Cream butter and sugar together until pale and creamy. Gradually beat in the eggs, a little at a time, beating well after each addition. Fold in flour, using a metal spoon. Mix the cocoa powder in a small bowl with some water to make a paste. Add this to the sponge mixture and fold in.

3 Spoon this mixture into the prepared cases and bake for 15–20 minutes until well risen and firm to the touch. Remove from the oven and transfer to a wire rack to cool.

4 In a small pan, slowly bring the cream to the boil. Remove from the heat and add the chocolate. Stir until the chocolate has melted. Return the mixture to the heat; bring to the boil, remove and cool.

5 When cool, ice the tops of the cupcakes with the ganache.

6 Break the white chocolate into pieces and place in a heatproof bowl over a pan of simmering water. Stir until it has melted. Pipe the white chocolate into a small circle in the middle of each cupcake. Add more circles around it. Drag a knife tip from the centre out, to the edge of the cupcake, and repeat several times to make a cobweb. Decorate with spider sweets.

Hanukkah cupcakes

Hanukkah is the Jewish Festival of Lights and one of the most enjoyable holidays of the Jewish calendar. It dates back to two centuries before the beginning of Christianity and usually occurs in December. Traditional foods celebrating this festival include potato latkes and doughnuts; this is my take on its sweet treats. Makes 12.

Ingredients

100g (4oz) unsalted butter
100g (4oz) caster sugar
2 eggs, beaten
100g (4oz) self-raising flour
4 tbsp strawberry jam

Topping

Double cream, whipped

Decoration

Mini-doughnuts

1   Pre-heat the oven to 180°C (350°F/Gas 4), then line a 12-hole bun tin with paper cases.

2   Cream the butter and sugar together until pale and creamy. Gradually beat in the eggs, a little at a time, beating well after each addition. Fold in the flour, using a metal spoon. Add the strawberry jam and, using a knife, drag through the mixture. You do not want to mix it in completely.

3   Spoon this mixture into the prepared cases and bake for 15–20 minutes until well risen and golden. Remove from the oven and transfer to a wire rack to cool.

4   Spoon the whipped cream on to the tops of the cupcakes and decorate with the mini-doughnuts.

New-baby cupcakes

No baby shower will be complete without these adorable cupcakes.
Makes 12.

Ingredients

100g (4oz) unsalted butter
100g (4oz) caster sugar
2 eggs, beaten
½ tsp vanilla essence
100g (4oz) self-raising flour

Topping
175g (7oz) icing sugar, sifted

1 egg white
½ tsp lemon juice
A couple of drops of blue or pink
food colouring

Decoration
Ready-rolled icing
Baby's bootee template
White, blue and pink writing icing

1 Pre-heat the oven to 180°C (350°F/Gas 4), then line a 12-hole bun tin with paper cases.

2 Cream the butter and sugar together until pale and creamy. Gradually beat in the eggs, a little at a time, beating well after each addition. Add the vanilla essence and mix well. Fold in the flour, using a metal spoon.

3 Spoon this mixture into the prepared cases and bake for 15–20 minutes until well risen and golden. Remove from the oven and transfer to a wire rack to cool.

4 For the topping, gradually add the sifted icing sugar to the egg white, beating as you go until it is thick and glossy. Add the lemon juice and a few drops of the appropriate food colouring and mix to create a pastel colour. Spoon onto the cooled cupcakes.

5 Roll out the icing to the correct thickness, and, using the template, cut out some bootee shapes. Use the writing icing to ice little dots over the bootee and ice on some laces. Using a palette knife, carefully position one or two of the booties on each cake.

Thanksgiving pumpkin cupcakes

In the USA, Thanksgiving is celebrated on the fourth Thursday in November each year. It is a time for family gatherings and holiday meals. Traditionally, a Thanksgiving meal includes roast turkey (and all of the trimmings), sweet potatoes and pumpkin pie. These pumpkin cupcakes make an excellent celebration treat. Makes 12.

Ingredients

125ml vegetable oil
75g caster sugar
50g light brown sugar
2 eggs
110g self-raising flour
½ teaspoon baking powder
½ teaspoon grated mixed spice
100g grated pumpkin

For the frosting:

100g unsalted butter, very soft
100g icing sugar
160g cream cheese
100g orange curd

1 Pre-heat the oven to 180°C (350°F/Gas 4). Peel the pumpkin, remove the seeds and then grate the flesh.

2 Sift the self-raising flour, baking powder and salt into a bowl. Add the mixed spice.

3 In another bowl add the sugars, vegetable oil and break in the eggs.

4 Mix the dry ingredients together so they are evenly distributed. Then whisk the wet ingredients together.

5 Mix the 150g of grated pumpkin into the oil mixture, the fold in the dry ingredients and stir it until it is free from lumps of flour.

6 Ladle the cake mixture into the cupcake cases, filling each one about two thirds of the way up. Put the cupcakes into the oven and bake them for 25 minutes, then remove them from the oven and leave them to cool completely.

7 To prepare the icing sift the icing sugar into a bowl and place in the soft butter. Whisk them together so there are no lumps, then add in the cream cheese and whisk it again until it is all smooth. Then add the orange curd. Whisk well together. Pipe or spoon the mixture onto the top of the cupcakes.

Index

Index